THE EUGÉNIE ROCHEROLLE SERIES

Intermediate Piano Solo

Continental Suite

6 Original Piano Solos by Eugénie Rocherolle

T0081927

2	Belgian Lace
6	La Piazza
10	Les Avenues de Paris
14	Oktoberfest
18	Rondo Capichio
22	In Old Vienna

ISBN 978-1-61780-582-0

HAL•LEONARD®
CORPORATION

7777 W. BLUEMOUND RD. P.O. BOX 13819 MILWAUKEE, WI 53213

In Australia Contact:
Hal Leonard Australia Pty. Ltd.
4 Lentara Court
Cheltenham, Victoria, 3192 Australia
Email: ausadmin@halleonard.com.au

Visit Hal Leonard Online at
www.halleonard.com

BELGIAN LACE
(La Dentelle de Belgique)

By EUGÉNIE ROCHEROLLE

Moderato (♩ = 120)

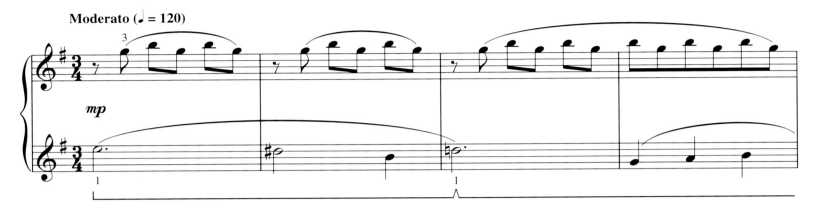

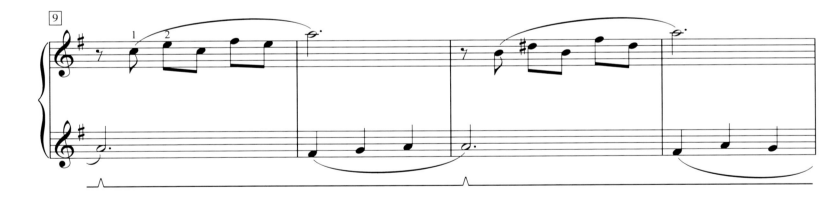

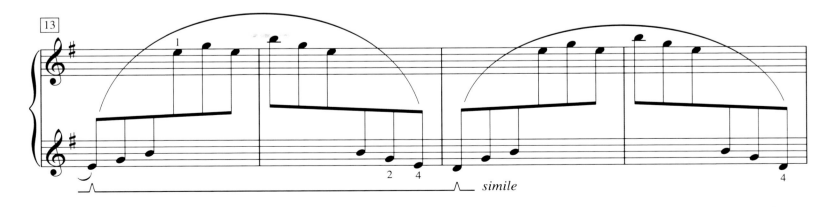

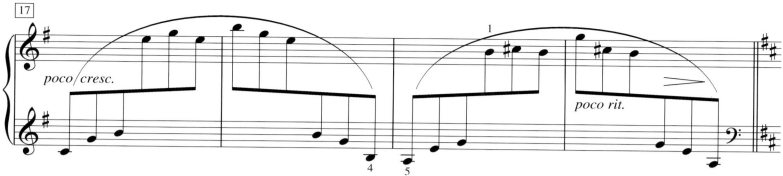

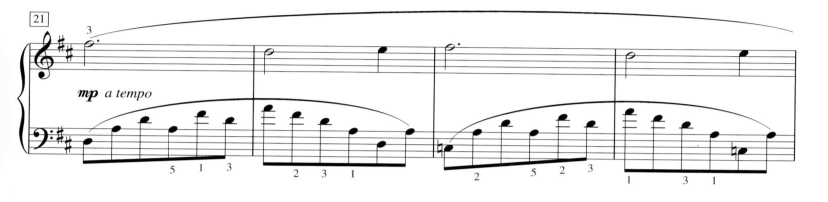

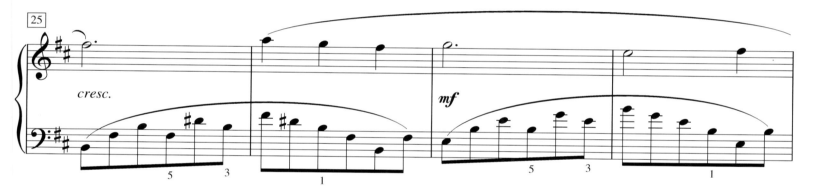

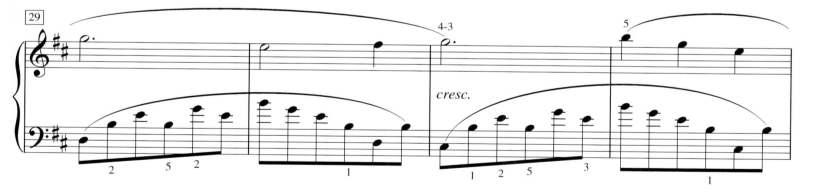

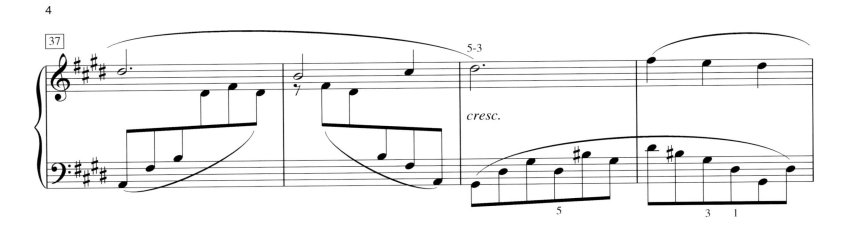

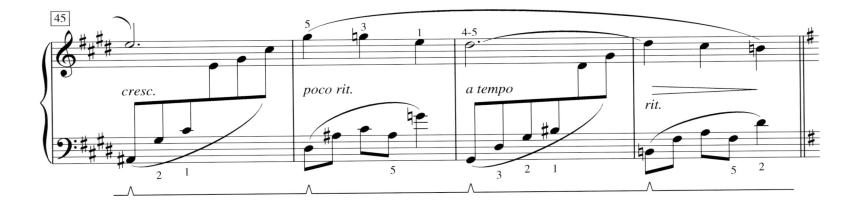

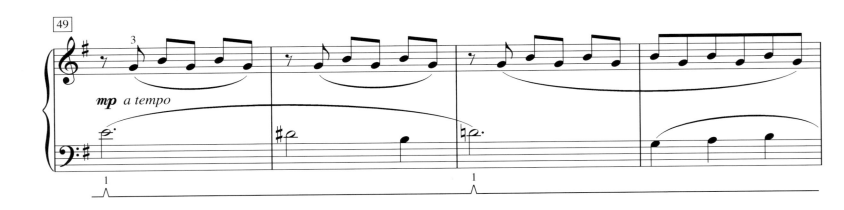

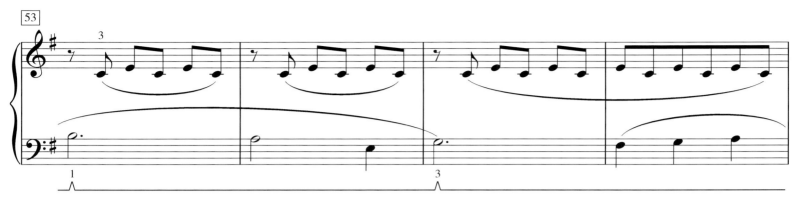

simile

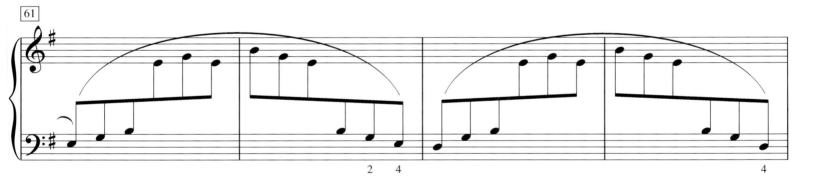

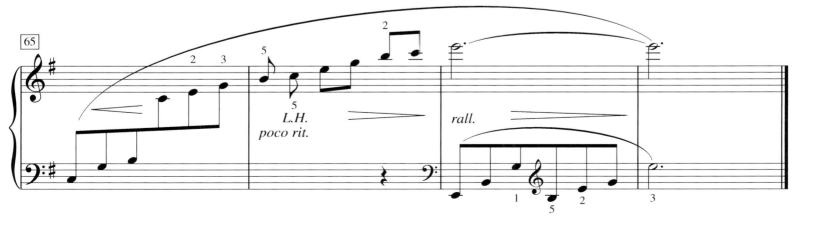

LA PIAZZA

By EUGÉNIE ROCHEROLLE

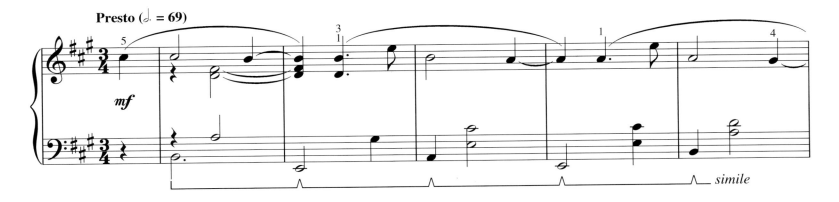

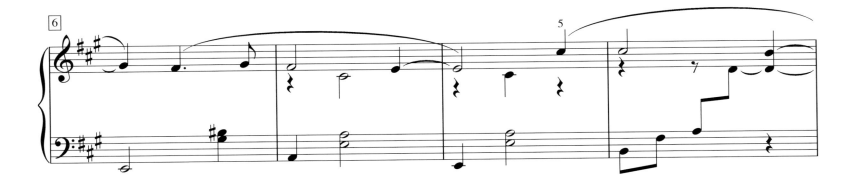

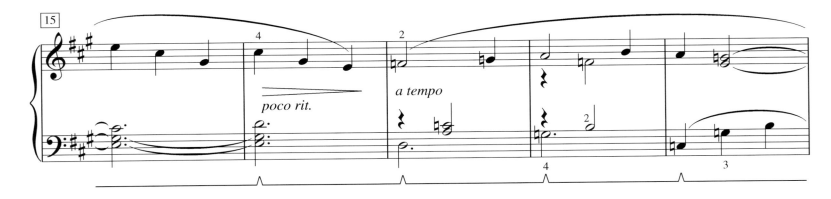

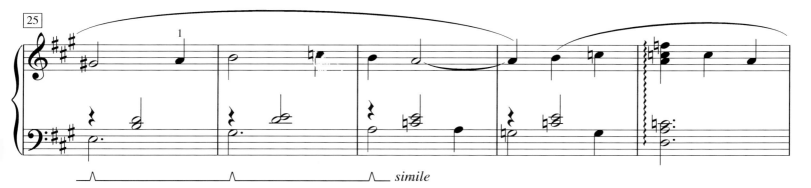

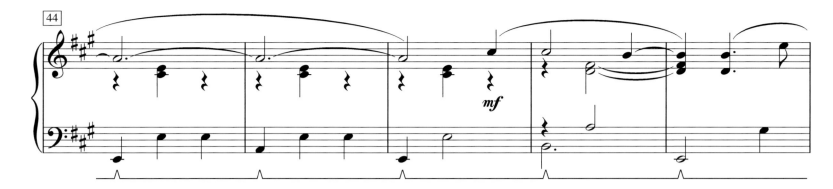

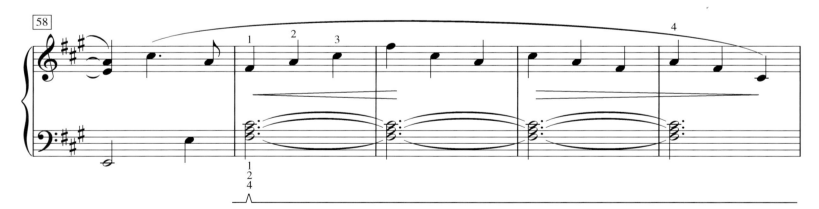

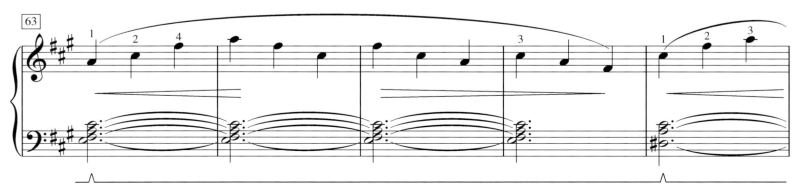

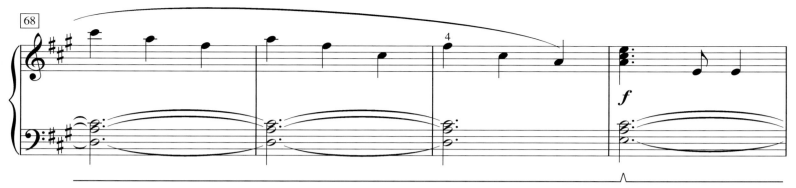

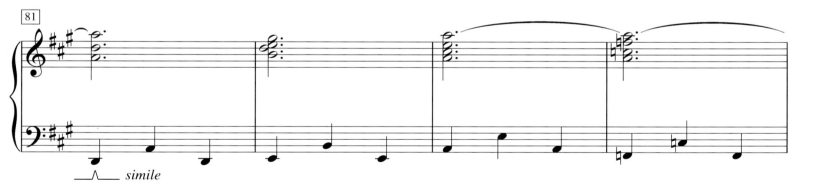

LES AVENUES DE PARIS

In memory of Billy VerPlanck

By EUGÉNIE ROCHEROLLE

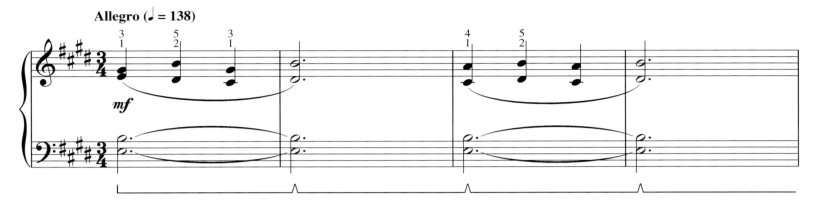

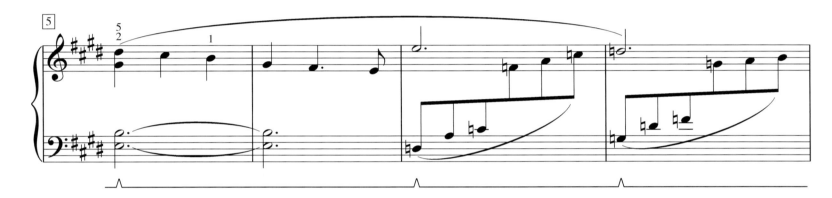

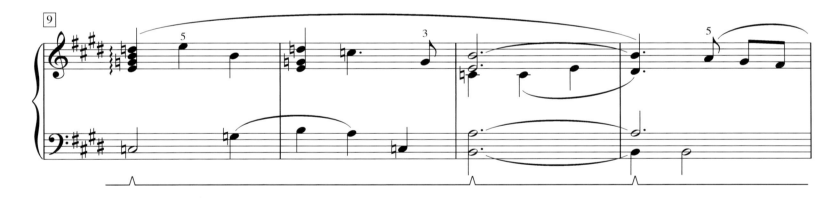

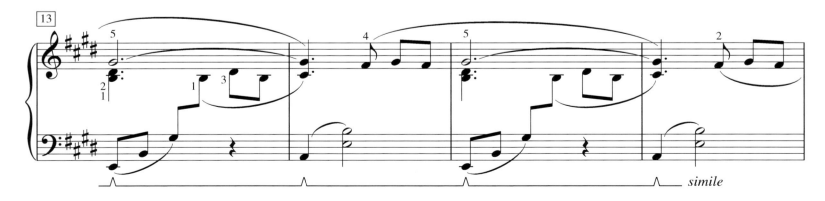

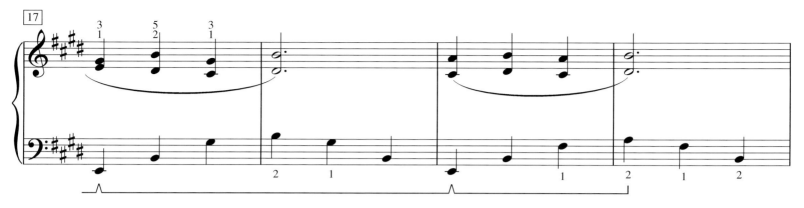

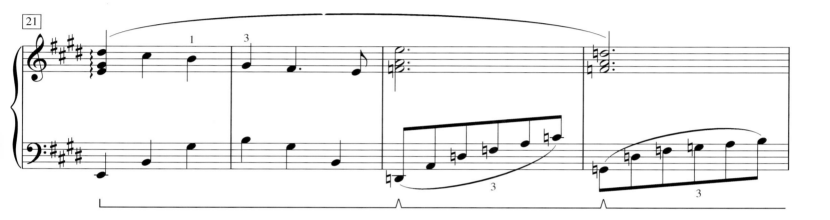

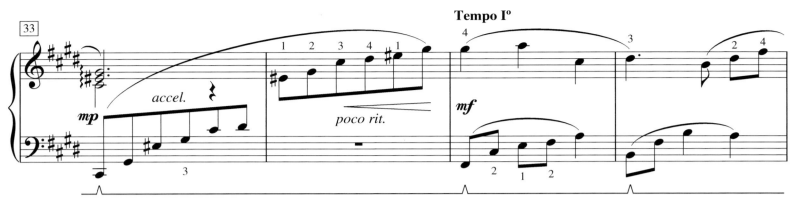

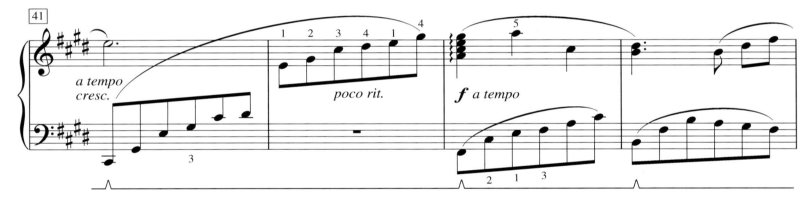

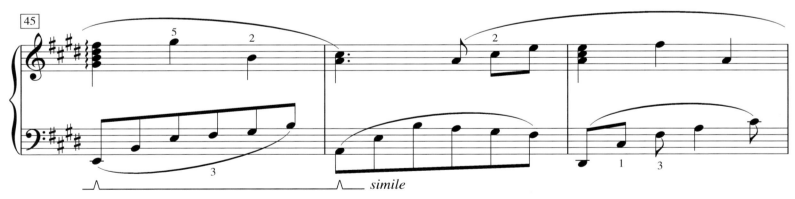

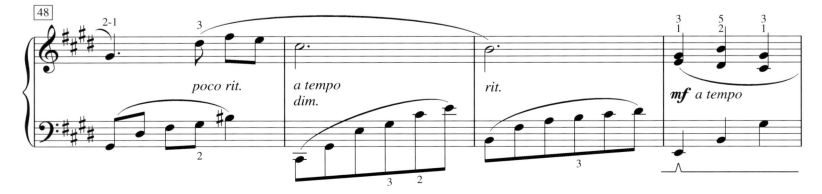

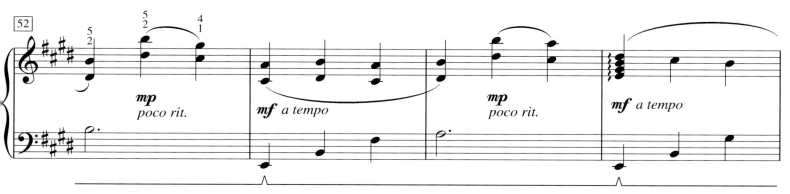

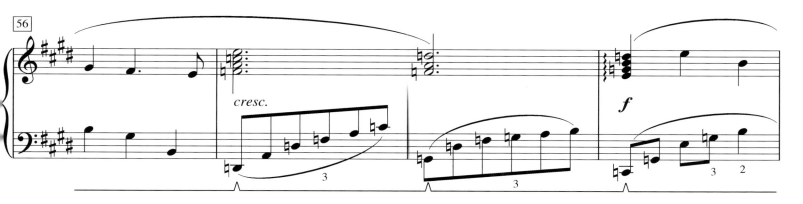

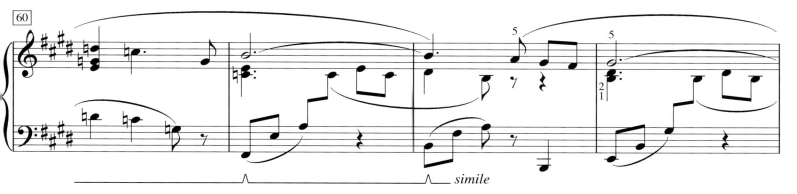

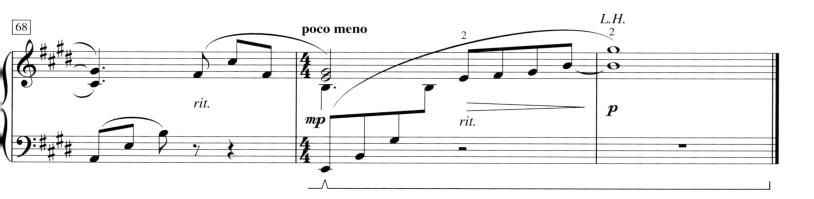

OKTOBERFEST

To Raford and Nancy Hulan

By EUGÉNIE ROCHEROLLE

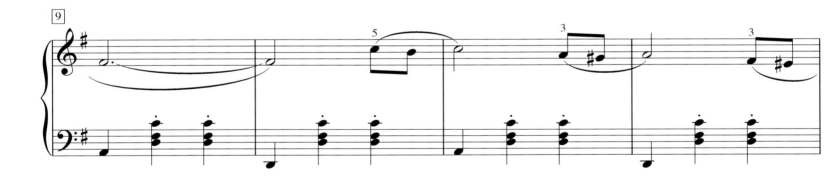

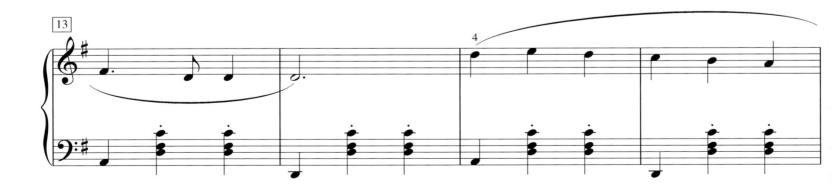

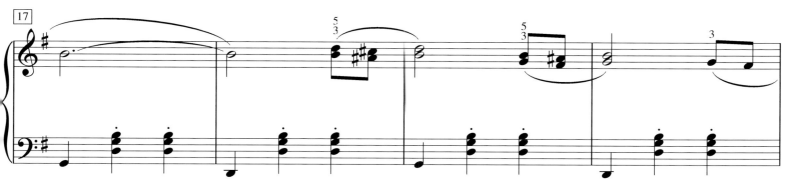

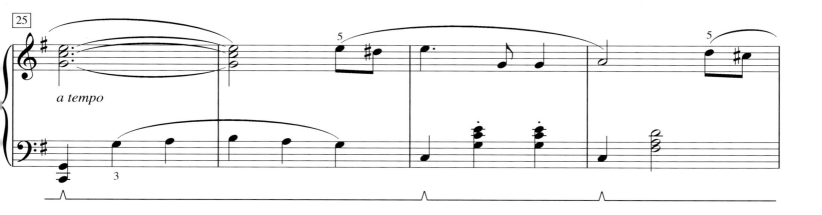

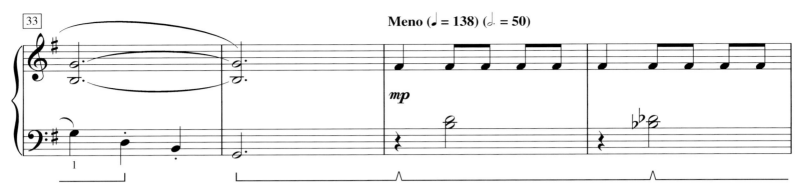

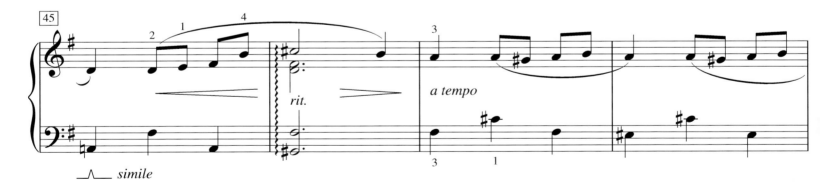

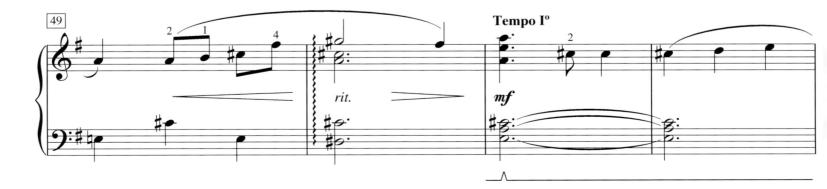

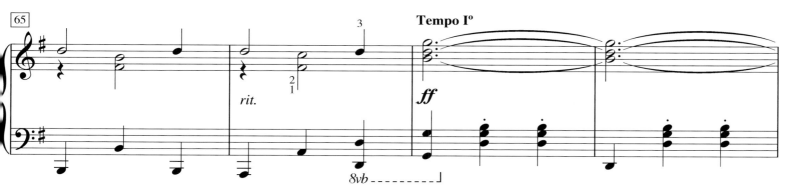

RONDO CAPICHIO

By EUGÉNIE ROCHEROLLE

Moderato (♩ = 112)

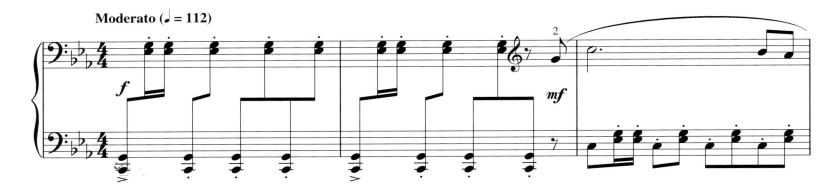

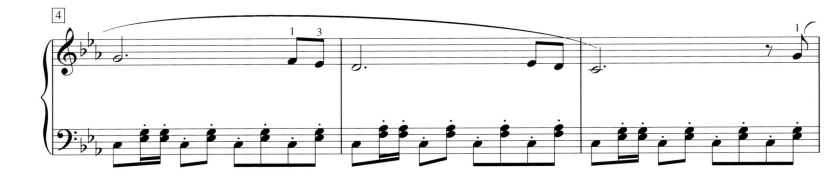

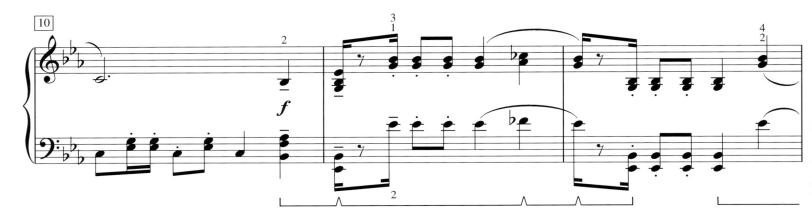

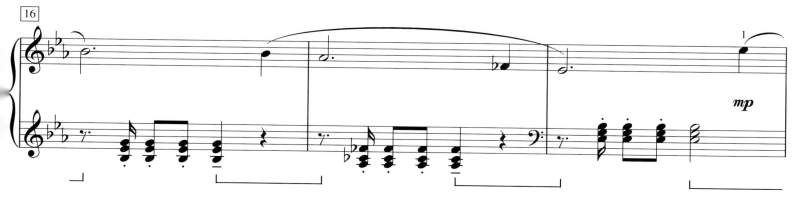

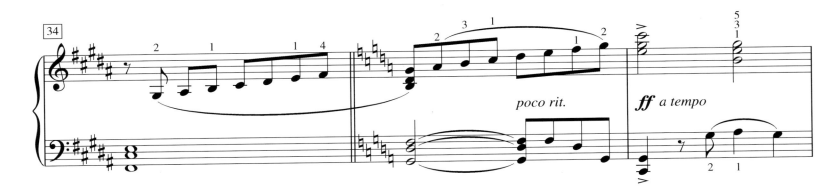

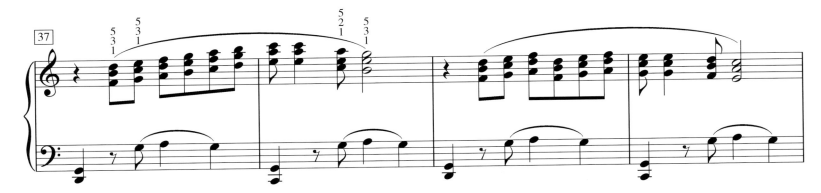

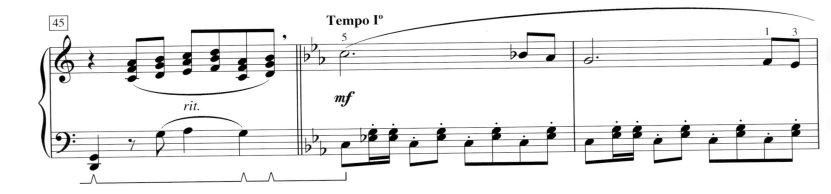

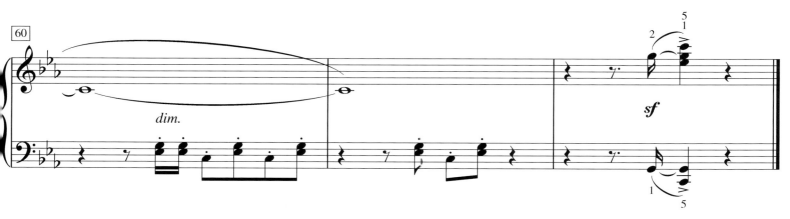

IN OLD VIENNA

To Cecelia M. Wyatt

By EUGÉNIE ROCHEROLLE

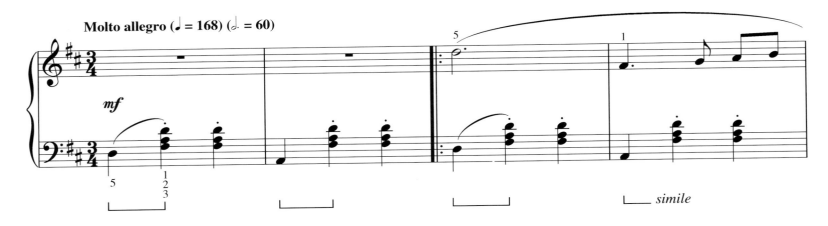

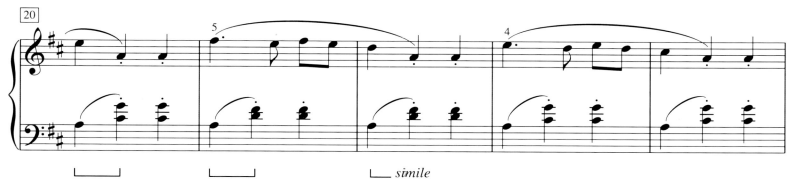

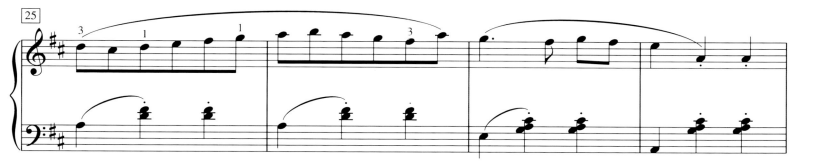

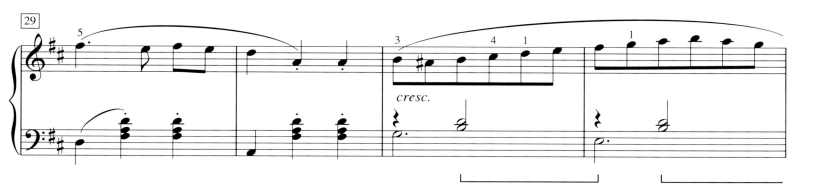

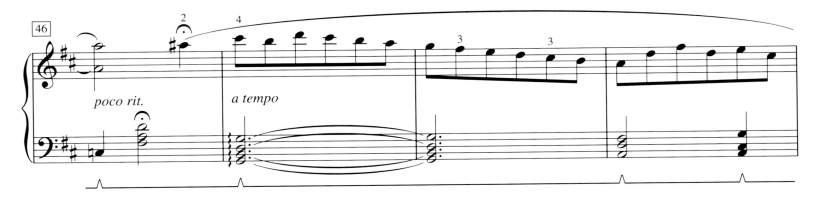

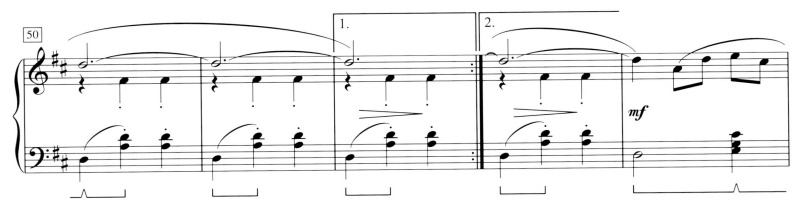

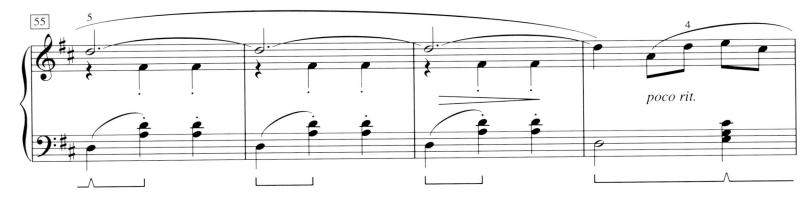